CREATIVE COOKING COLLECTION

High Fibre Cooking

A&P

CREATIVE COOKING COLLECTION

High Fibre Cooking

Carole Handslip

CONTENTS

Published exclusively for Cupress (Canada) Limited
10 Falconer Drive, Unit 8, Mississauga,
Ontario L5N 1B1, Canada
by Woodhead-Faulkner Ltd

First published 1988
© Woodhead-Faulkner (Publishers) Ltd 1988
All rights reserved
ISBN 0-920691-22-6
Printed and bound in Italy by Arnoldo Mondadori Editore

INTRODUCTION

For centuries people have gone to excessive lengths to remove the fibre—or roughage, as it is also known—from the food we eat. Since Roman times millers have refined away the fibre from most of our flour to make bread as 'pure and white' as possible. So why the sudden change of heart? What is it that has transformed our thinking about fibre? What is this fibre anyway?

Fibre is an indigestible fibrous material which occurs naturally in plant foods. It is not found in animal foods. Fibre has no apparent nutritional value, for it passes through our systems virtually unchanged, yet it is an extremely valuable material, for it greatly assists the movement of foods through our digestive systems.

A simple study of the African villager's state of health shows just how valuable fibre is. Diseases such as constipation, cancer of the bowel, diverticulitis and many other 'Western ailments' that plague us in later life are relatively unknown amongst African village dwellers. The staple food in Africa is maize, supplemented by root crops, fruits, nuts and grains—all rich in dietary fibre. But submit the African villager to our Western diet and he finds himself prone to those 'Western diseases'.

Most experts now agree that the typical Western diet is deficient in fibre, a factor which can be detrimental to health. High fibre foods benefit us in many ways. First, fibre adds bulk to our food, giving us a sense of fullness, without having consumed a large amount of calories. So foods rich in fibre can play an important role in a calorie-controlled diet.

Fibre makes food travel faster through the intestines, exercising the lower digestive tract, reducing pressure, preventing constipation and diluting potentially harmful toxic waste substances. Another bonus is that foods rich in dietary fibre tend to be low in saturated fat, which is associated at high levels with heart disease and related disorders.

All of us eat some fibre; most of us simply don't eat nearly enough. It's not a question of rushing out to stock up with a range of new, way out foods; it's more a need to alter the balance of our eating habits.

Start by introducing wholegrain cereals at breakfast time, or make your own granola or muesli. Bake your own bread from whole wheat flour if you possibly can. Once a week I make a batch of loaves and freeze them for use during the week. If you haven't time to do this, make sure you buy whole wheat bread. Introduce a wide variety of beans, pulses and grains, vegetables and fruits, and you will certainly be increasing your fibre intake. If you also cut down on refined foods, especially sugar, add less salt to food and eat less fat, particularly animal fat, you will undoubtedly enjoy a healthier diet.

COOKING RICE & PULSES

BROWN RICE

Brown rice has an interesting nutty flavour and a chewier texture than white rice. The reason for this is that unlike white rice, brown rice has not been stripped of its fibre, the rich outer coat which also supplies us with valuable vitamins, particularly Thiamin B_1. You can buy brown long-grain, short-grain, Basmati and easy-cook Italian rice. I think Basmati is the most delicious but it is also the most expensive.

Brown rice is straightforward to cook; it is far less likely to go mushy than white rice, though it does entail a longer cooking time. There are two main methods of cooking brown rice; the first minimizes the loss of vitamins.

Allow 50 ml (¼ cup) rice per person.

Cooking Method 1

1. Wash the rice well and drain.
2. Place in a saucepan and add approximately 200 ml (¾ cup) boiling water and a pinch of salt for each 50 ml (¼ cup) rice. Bring back to the boil, cover and simmer for 35–40 minutes.
3. Check after 30 minutes to make sure it is not too dry; add a little more water if necessary.
4. By the end of the cooking time, the water should have been completely absorbed and the rice should be dry and fluffy. If not, uncover and cook for 1 minute to drive off the excess moisture.

Cooking Method 2

1. Cook the rice in plenty of boiling salted water for 35–40 minutes.
2. Drain, rinse well, drain again and turn into a warmed shallow dish. Leave in a warm place for a few minutes to steam dry.

PULSES

This is the collective name for beans, peas and lentils. They are cheap to buy, keep well and are the basis of many interesting dishes, often originating from the Middle East and South America. It can be difficult to get your family to start eating beans and lentils. My advice is to introduce them gradually, first in the familiar dishes such as chilli con carne, lentil soup and minestrone. After a while, the family will accept them in their more adventurous guises.

Beans are one of the richest sources of fibre; they have a high protein content and are also rich in iron, potassium and the B vitamins. When sprouted, they have the added bonus of vitamin C. One common objection to pulses is that they cause flatulence. To counter this problem, introduce them in your diet gradually and take care with their cooking. Drain off the water in which they are soaked, as this contains the substances which cause flatulence.

All dried beans and peas need to be soaked for about 8 hours, or overnight, before cooking. Alternatively, cook them in boiling water for 2 minutes, then remove from the heat and leave to soak for 2 hours. Lentils and split peas do not need to be pre-soaked before cooking, though it will shorten the cooking time if they are.

For convenience and to save fuel, I tend to cook large quantities of beans when I have the time, bag them in 125 ml (½ cup) or 250 ml (1 cup) quantities and freeze for future use; you can also store them in the refrigerator for 2–3 days.

Cooking Method
1. Drain the beans, place in a pan and add about 4 times their volume of fresh water; bring to the boil. Boil rapidly for 10 minutes to destroy any harmful toxins that may be present, skimming off any scum.
2. Reduce the heat, cover and simmer for the required cooking time (see page 79). Add salt, if desired, towards the end of cooking as it toughens the skin and lengthens the cooking time if added sooner.

NUTS AND SEEDS
One of the easiest and most delicious ways of increasing the fibre content of both sweet and savoury dishes is to add seeds or nuts to them. The flavour of the nuts and seeds is even richer (and I find more delicious) when you roast them. Cool and add to salads, fruit dishes, muesli and savoury dishes.

To brown sunflower seeds, sesame seeds and pumpkin seeds
Place the seeds in a dry heavy-based pan with a tight-fitting lid. Shake the pan over a moderate heat for about 1 minute or until the seeds begin to pop and turn golden brown.

To brown nuts
Chop the nuts if you prefer, then sprinkle them in a single layer on a baking sheet. Place in a preheated oven, 190°/375°F, for about 10 minutes or until golden brown. If you are in a hurry, place the nuts under a broiler for 4–5 minutes and turn frequently.

NOTES

Ingredients are given in both metric and imperial measures. Use either set of quantities but not a mixture of both in any one recipe.

All spoon measurements are level:
1 tablespoon = one 15 ml spoon
1 teaspoon = one 5 ml spoon.

Ovens should be preheated to the temperature specified.

Freshly ground black pepper is intended where pepper is listed.

Eggs are large size unless otherwise stated.

Fresh herbs are used unless otherwise stated. If unobtainable, dried herbs can be substituted in cooked dishes but halve the quantities.

If fresh yeast is unobtainable, substitute dried yeast but halve the quantity and use according to the manufacturer's directions.

Basic recipes are marked with an asterisk and given in the reference section (pages 74–7). Increase or decrease the basic quantities in proportion to obtain the amount required.

BREAKFAST DISHES

KEDGEREE

A really tasty breakfast. Cook the rice the night before then it will only take you a few minutes to assemble and heat through. I prefer to use Finnan haddock as it is free from artificial colouring and has an excellent flavour.

Serves 4
Preparation time:
15 minutes, plus cooking rice
Cooking time:
5 minutes
Freezing:
Not recommended

125 ml (1/2 cup) brown rice, cooked
2 hard-boiled eggs, chopped
1 tablespoon chopped parsley

250 g (8 oz) Finnan haddock, poached and flaked
2 tablespoons yogurt
salt and pepper to taste

1. Place the rice, eggs, parsley, fish, and salt and pepper in a pan. Mix together, then heat through gently, stirring.
2. Stir in the yogurt and serve immediately.

SUNRISE SUNDAE

A fresh start to the day, but a little more filling than the citrus fruits usually served at breakfast.

125 g (4 oz) dried apricots
125 g (4 oz) pitted prunes
450 ml (1 3/4 cups) water
2 oranges

4 tablespoons yogurt
4 tablespoons Granola (page 10)

Serves 4
Preparation time:
10 minutes
Cooking time:
15 minutes
Freezing:
Not recommended

1. Place the apricots, prunes and water in a saucepan and bring to the boil. Cover and simmer for 15 minutes, then leave to cool, with the lid on the pan.
2. Peel the oranges and divide into segments, discarding all the pith and pips. Mix with the other fruit, then turn into 4 individual shallow dishes.
3. Top each with a spoonful of yogurt, then sprinkle with a spoonful of granola.

RASPBERRY YOGURT DRINK

Refreshing and filling—ideal when you're in a hurry. Substitute blackberries, when in season, as they are very high in fibre. Experiment with other fruits of your choice —for sweeter fruits you will probably need less honey.

Makes 450 ml (1¾ cups)
Preparation time: 5 minutes
Freezing: Not recommended

50 g (2 oz) raspberries
150 ml (²/₃ cup) yogurt

125 ml (½ cup) milk
2 teaspoons liquid honey

1. Place all the ingredients in a blender or food processor, and work until smooth.
2. Pour into glasses to serve.

GRANOLA

A scrumptious cereal to serve at breakfast time with milk or natural yogurt and fruit. Alter the cereals, nuts and seeds according to what you have available. Coconut gives it an interesting flavour for a change.
    I particularly like to serve granola with apricot purée —made simply by cooking 150 g (5 oz) dried apricots in 300 ml (1¼ cups) water for 20 minutes, then working in a blender or food processor until smooth.

3 tablespoons sunflower
*   oil*
4 tablespoons malt extract
1 tablespoon liquid honey
150 ml (²/₃ cup) rolled oats
150 ml (²/₃ cup) jumbo oats

75 g (3 oz) buckwheat
*   flakes*
50 g (2 oz) hazelnuts,
*   chopped*
50 ml (¼ cup) sunflower
*   seeds*
2 tablespoons sesame seeds

Makes 550 ml (2¼ cups)
Preparation time: 15 minutes
Cooking time: 30–35 minutes
Freezing: Not recommended

1. Place the oil, malt extract and honey in a large saucepan and heat gently until the malt is runny.
2. Stir in the remaining ingredients and mix thoroughly.
3. Turn the mixture into a large roasting pan and bake in a preheated oven, 180°C/350°F, for 30–35 minutes, stirring occasionally so that it browns evenly.
4. Leave to cool, breaking up the granola to separate the pieces as it does so. Store in an airtight container.

VARIATION
Mix together 250 ml (1 cup) granola, 300 ml (1¼ cups) natural yogurt, and 1 sliced banana or 2 sliced peaches and divide between 4 individual bowls.

CORN FRITTERS

So quick to make that you don't need to get up before anyone else in the family. Vary the fritters by adding cooked diced bacon, chopped green onions or herbs.

2 tablespoons whole wheat flour
1 egg
3 tablespoons milk
50 g (2 oz) Cheddar cheese, grated

198 g (7 oz) can kernel corn, drained
salt and pepper to taste
oil for shallow-frying

Makes 6
Preparation time:
15 minutes
Cooking time:
8 minutes
Freezing:
Not recommended

1. Place the flour in a mixing bowl, make a well in the centre and drop in the egg. Add the milk and mix, gradually incorporating the flour; beat until smooth.
2. Mix in the cheese, corn, and salt and pepper.
3. Heat the oil in a frying pan, add tablespoonfuls of the mixture and fry for 2 minutes on each side, until golden brown. Repeat with remaining batter.

BREAKFAST SCONES

Very quick to make fresh for breakfast. Serve with sweet or savoury toppings: try cottage cheese with chopped dates, banana or apple if you want a sweet topping; cooked diced bacon or green onions for a savoury one.

500 ml (2 cups) whole wheat flour
1 teaspoon cream of tartar, sifted
½ teaspoon baking soda, sifted

pinch of salt
50 ml (¼ cup) margarine
125 ml (½ cup) milk (approximately)
¼ teaspoon poppy seeds
milk to glaze

Makes 5
Preparation time:
15 minutes
Cooking time:
12–15 minutes
Freezing:
Recommended

1. Place all the ingredients, except the poppy seeds, in a mixing bowl and mix with a fork to form a soft dough, adding a little more milk if necessary.
2. Turn onto a lightly floured surface, knead lightly and roll out to a 2 cm (¾ inch) thickness. Cut into 7.5 cm (3 inch) rounds with a plain cutter.
3. Place on a floured baking sheet, brush with milk and sprinkle with the poppy seeds.
4. Bake in a preheated oven, 220°C/425°F, for 12–15 minutes.
5. Transfer to a wire rack to cool.

MUESLI

The base mixture can be varied daily by adding grated apple or other fresh fruits. Use apple juice instead of milk for a change, and add yogurt.

175 g (6 oz) rolled oats
125 g (4 oz) wheat flakes
125 g (4 oz) barley flakes
75 g (3 oz) hazelnuts,
chopped and browned
75 g (3 oz) raisins

75 g (3 oz) chopped dates
25 g (1 oz) dried apple,
chopped
2 tablespoons dark
brown sugar

Makes: 750 g
(1½ lb)
Preparation time:
15 minutes
Freezing: Not
recommended

1. Mix all the ingredients together in a large bowl. Store in an airtight container and use as required.

FRUIT WITH HAZELNUT SAUCE

A lovely breakfast to serve in the summer when there are so many fresh fruits available. Choose several types, thinking about their colour, so they will look attractive on the plate. Serve with whole wheat bread.

50 g (2 oz) hazelnuts, browned
50 ml (¼ cup) whole wheat breadcrumbs
1 tablespoon liquid honey
1 tablespoon lemon juice

175 g (6 oz) yogurt (approximately)
selection of fresh fruits in season (e.g. pineapple, watermelon, peaches, apples, oranges, pears)

Serves 4
Preparation time:
20–30 minutes
Freezing:
Recommended for sauce only

1. Grind the hazelnuts finely in a food processor.
2. Add the remaining ingredients, except the fruit, and blend until smooth; add extra yogurt to thin if necessary.
3. Prepare the chosen fruits as necessary, slice and arrange on individual plates, then spoon a little hazelnut sauce onto each plate.

WAFFLES

These waffles are light and airy, and delicious served with fruit purée or strawberries and yogurt. It is well worth investing in the special waffle iron needed to make them.

*150 ml (²/₃ cup) whole
    wheat flour
1 teaspoon cinnamon
1 ¹/₂ teaspoons baking
    powder*

*1 egg, separated
1 teaspoon liquid honey
1 tablespoon oil
250 ml (1 cup) milk*

1. Place the flour in a mixing bowl and sift in the cinnamon and baking powder. Make a well in the centre.
2. Add the egg yolk, honey, oil and milk and beat until completely smooth.
3. Whisk the egg white until fairly stiff, then fold carefully into the batter.
4. Spoon a quarter of the mixture into a heated and oiled non-stick waffle iron and cook for 2–3 minutes on each side, until crisp and golden. Remove and keep warm.
5. Cook the remaining batter in the same way.

Makes 4
Preparation time:
10 minutes
Cooking time:
8–12 minutes
Freezing:
Recommended

BEAN AND TOMATO SOUP

A hearty, warming soup. For a quicker soup, use two 398 ml (14 oz) cans of drained white kidney beans instead of the dried beans; reduce the water to 900 ml (3⅔ cups) and the cooking time to 30 minutes.

2 tablespoons oil
1 large onion, chopped
2 celery sticks, chopped
2 cloves garlic, crushed
250 ml (1 cup) haricot or
* white beans, soaked*
* overnight*
1 bouquet garni

1 tablespoon tomato paste
398 ml (14 oz) can
* tomatoes*
1.2 litres (5 cups) water
2 teaspoons lemon juice
2 tablespoons chopped
* parsley*
salt and pepper to taste

Serves 6–8
Preparation time:
10 minutes
Cooking time:
2 hours
Freezing:
Recommended

1. Heat the oil in a pan, add the onion and celery and fry until softened.
2. Add the garlic, drained beans, bouquet garni, tomato paste, tomatoes and water. Bring to the boil, cover and simmer for about 2 hours, until the beans are tender, adding salt and pepper towards the end of cooking time.
3. Remove the bouquet garni. Add the lemon juice and parsley, check the seasoning and pour into a warmed soup tureen.

CURRIED LENTIL SOUP

1 onion, chopped
1 celery stick, chopped
1 carrot, chopped
1 clove garlic, crushed
175 ml (¾ cup) red lentils
900 ml (3⅔ cups) water

1 teaspoon curry powder
1 teaspoon turmeric
salt and pepper to taste
1 tablespoon chopped
* parsley to garnish*

Serves 4–6
Preparation time:
10 minutes
Cooking time:
45 minutes
Freezing:
Recommended

1. Place all the ingredients, except the salt and pepper, in a large saucepan. Bring to the boil, cover and simmer for 45 minutes, stirring occasionally.
2. Add salt and pepper, pour into a warmed soup tureen and sprinkle with the parsley to serve.

RED PEPPER SOUP

A light, refreshing soup—delicious hot or cold with crunchy curls of Whole wheat Melba Toast (page 22) or Poppy Seed Rolls (page 72).

4 red peppers
1 tablespoon sunflower oil
1 onion, chopped
1 clove garlic, crushed
600 ml (2½ cups) water

450 ml (1¾ cups) tomato
juice
salt and pepper to taste
4 tablespoons yogurt to
garnish

Serves 4
Preparation time:
25 minutes
Freezing:
Recommended

1. Plunge the red peppers into a pan of boiling water and leave to stand for 4 minutes. Drain.
2. Halve and core the peppers, removing all the seeds. Chop the flesh roughly and place in a food processor or blender.
3. Heat the oil in a pan, add the onion and fry until softened. Add the garlic and fry for 1 minute.
4. Add to the food processor or blender with the water and work until smooth.
5. Mix with the tomato juice and season with salt and pepper. Chill until required. If serving hot, heat through gently.
6. Pour into individual soup bowls and swirl a spoonful of yogurt into each one.

ICED LETTUCE SOUP

A delicately flavoured soup—an ideal way to use up tough outer leaves or lettuces that may have bolted in your garden. It can be served hot if you prefer.

1 tablespoon oil
1 onion, chopped
2 large lettuces, shredded
2 tablespoons whole
* wheat flour*

750 ml (3 cups) milk
pinch of grated nutmeg
150 ml (2/3 cup) table
* cream*
salt and pepper to taste

1. Heat the oil in a pan, add the onion and lettuce, cover and cook gently for about 8 minutes.
2. Remove from the heat and stir in the flour. Bring the milk to the boil, then gradually add to the pan, stirring constantly. Add salt, pepper and nutmeg, cover and simmer for 20 minutes.
3. Cool the soup, then purée in a food processor or blender until smooth.
4. Stir in three quarters of the table cream, then place in the refrigerator to chill. If serving hot, heat through gently, without boiling.
5. Pour into individual soup bowls and swirl the remaining cream into each one. Serve with Whole wheat Melba Toast (page 22) or Poppy Seed Rolls (page 72).

Serves 4
Preparation time:
10 minutes
Cooking time:
30 minutes
Freezing:
Recommended

MINTED MELON SALAD

A wonderful combination of flavours that makes a light, refreshing first course and excites the appetite.

1 small honeydew melon,   *¼ cucumber*
   halved   *2 teaspoons lemon juice*
125 g (4 oz) strawberries,   *1 tablespoon olive oil*
   sliced   *pepper to taste*
1 tablespoon chopped mint

Serves 4
Preparation time:
15 minutes, plus marinating
Freezing:
Not recommended

1. Scoop out the seeds from the melon and discard. Cut off the skin, then cut the melon into 1 cm (½ inch) pieces or scoop into balls, using a melon baller.
2. Place the melon in a bowl with the strawberries and sprinkle with the mint.
3. Slice the cucumber, then cut the slices into quarters. Add to the bowl.
4. Mix the lemon juice, oil and pepper together, pour over the salad and toss until well coated.
5. Leave for 30 minutes for the flavours to combine, then serve in individual dishes.

PROVENÇALE SALAD

1 small egg plant, sliced   *4 tomatoes, sliced*
4 tablespoons olive oil   *2 tablespoons chopped*
250 g (8 oz) zucchini,   *parsley*
   sliced   *50 g (2 oz) black olives,*
1 red pepper, cored, seeded   *halved and pitted*
   and sliced   *1 tablespoon lemon juice*
2 cloves garlic, crushed   *salt and pepper to taste*

Serves 6
Preparation time:
15 minutes, plus standing and cooling time
Cooking time:
20 minutes
Freezing:
Recommended, without the tomatoes

1. Place the egg plant slices in a colander, sprinkle with salt and leave for 30 minutes. Rinse well and pat dry with paper towels.
2. Heat half the oil in a frying pan, add the egg plant slices and fry on both sides until pale golden. Place in a bowl.
3. Add the remaining oil to the pan and fry the zucchini and red pepper for 8–10 minutes, stirring occasionally, until softened.
4. Add the garlic, and salt and pepper; fry for 2 minutes.
5. Add to the egg plant with the tomatoes, parsley, olives and lemon juice and toss thoroughly. Leave to cool, then transfer to a shallow serving dish and serve with Poppy Seed Rolls (page 72).

CASHEW NUT PÂTÉ

1 tablespoon oil
50 g (2 oz) mushrooms,
chopped
1 clove garlic, crushed
125 g (4 oz) cashew nuts,
roasted
handful parsley

125 ml (¼ cup) cooked
pinto beans
2 tablespoons yogurt
salt and pepper to taste
radish slices to garnish

Serves 4–6
Preparation time:
15 minutes, plus
cooking beans
Freezing:
Recommended

1. Heat the oil in a pan, add the mushrooms and garlic and fry for 2–3 minutes, stirring occasionally. Set aside.
2. Place the nuts and parsley in a food processor or blender and chop. Add the beans and yogurt and work until smooth.
3. Turn the mixture into a bowl, add the mushrooms, and salt and pepper and mix well.
4. Turn into a serving dish, garnish with the radish slices and serve with Whole wheat Melba Toast (see below).

MUSHROOM PÂTÉ

1 tablespoon sunflower oil
1 onion, chopped
175 g (6 oz) mushrooms,
chopped
2 cloves garlic, crushed
125 ml (½ cup) cooked
butter beans

2 tablespoons chopped
parsley
¼ teaspoon chopped
thyme
salt and pepper to taste
thyme sprigs to garnish

Serves 4
Preparation time:
15 minutes, plus
cooking beans
Cooking time:
10 minutes
Freezing:
Recommended

1. Heat the oil in a pan, add the onion and fry until softened.
2. Add the mushrooms and garlic and fry for 5 minutes, stirring occasionally.
3. Purée the beans and herbs in a food processor or blender.
4. Mix with the mushroom mixture and season with salt and pepper. Turn into a serving dish and garnish with thyme. Serve with Whole wheat Melba Toast (see below).

WHOLE WHEAT MELBA TOAST
Simply toast a slice of whole wheat bread on both sides. Place on a flat surface, cut off the crusts and, holding your hand firmly on top, split the slice horizontally with a knife, using a sawing action. Place under a preheated broiler, cut sides up, until the toasts curl up and turn golden.

SUNFLOWER-STUFFED POTATOES

2 large potatoes
125 g (4 oz) Cheddar
    cheese, grated
3 tablespoons yogurt

6 green onions, chopped
50 g (2 oz) toasted
    sunflower seeds,
    chopped
salt and pepper to taste

Serves 4
Preparation time:
10 minutes
Cooking time:
1½ hours
Freezing:
Recommended

1. Make a slit along one side of each potato and bake in a preheated oven, 200°C/400°F, for 1¼ hours or until cooked.
2. Halve the potatoes lengthways, scoop out the flesh into a bowl and mash with half the cheese, the yogurt, green onions, sunflower seeds, and salt and pepper.
3. Spoon the mixture into the potato shells, sprinkle with the remaining cheese and return to the oven for 15 minutes or until golden.

CHEESE AND CORN FLAN

1 tablespoon oil
1 onion, chopped
1 celery stick, chopped
1 clove garlic, crushed
2 eggs
150 ml (⅔ cup) milk
175 ml (¾ cup) frozen
    kernel corn

125 g (4 oz) Cheddar
    cheese, grated
2 tablespoons chopped
    parsley
¾ batch Whole wheat
    Pastry*
salt and pepper to taste

Serves 4–6
Preparation time:
20 minutes, plus
pastry making
Cooking time:
45 minutes
Freezing:
Recommended

1. Heat the oil in a pan, add the onion, celery and garlic and fry until softened.
2. Beat the eggs and milk together in a bowl, then stir in the corn, onion mixture, cheese, parsley, and salt and pepper.
3. Roll out the pastry thinly and use to line a 20 cm (8 inch) flan or quiche pan.
4. Spoon in the filling and bake in a preheated oven, 200°C/400°F, for 30 minutes. Lower the heat to 190°C/375°F and cook for 15 minutes. Serve warm or cold.

CHEESE ROULADE

A very impressive dish to serve with a crisp salad for a summer lunch. It is equally good eaten cold. It also makes an attractive first course served with Tomato Sauce*.

125 ml (½ cup) whole wheat
  breadcrumbs
75 g (3 oz) Cheddar
  cheese, grated
25 g (1 oz) Parmesan
  cheese, grated
125 g (4 oz) Ricotta
  cheese
4 eggs, separated
½ teaspoon dry mustard
salt and pepper to taste

FOR THE FILLING:
1 tablespoon oil
1 onion, chopped
250 g (8 oz) frozen
  chopped spinach,
  thawed and drained
125 g (4 oz) Ricotta
  cheese
good pinch of grated
  nutmeg

Serves 4
Preparation time:
20 minutes
Cooking time:
10–15 minutes
Freezing:
Not recommended

1. Line and grease a 30 × 20 cm (12 × 8 inch) jelly roll pan.
2. Place the breadcrumbs, Cheddar cheese, all but 1 tablespoon of the Parmesan cheese, the Ricotta, egg yolks, mustard, and salt and pepper in a bowl and mix well.
3. Whisk the egg whites until fairly stiff, then carefully fold into the cheese mixture with a metal spoon.
4. Turn the mixture into the prepared pan and bake in a preheated oven, 200°C/400°F, for 10–15 minutes, until risen and firm.
5. Meanwhile, prepare the filling. Heat the oil in a pan, add the onion and fry until softened. Add the spinach and cook, stirring, for 5 minutes.
6. Add the Ricotta, nutmeg, and salt and pepper and heat through gently.
7. Sprinkle the remaining Parmesan cheese over a sheet of waxed paper. Turn the roulade out onto the paper and peel off the lining paper.
8. Spread with the filling and roll up like a jelly roll. Serve immediately in slices.

VARIATIONS

Mushroom Filling: Add 175 g (6 oz) thinly sliced mushrooms in place of the spinach and fry for 5 minutes. Continue as above.

Kernel corn Filling: Add 125 ml (½ cup) cooked kernel corn instead of the spinach and heat through gently before adding the Ricotta and seasonings.

TAGLIATELLE WITH OLIVE SAUCE

*500 g (1 lb) fresh
    wholewheat tagliatelle
FOR THE SAUCE:
1 tablespoon olive oil
1 onion, sliced
1 red pepper, cored, seeded
    and sliced
2 cloves garlic, crushed*

*398 ml (14 oz) can
    tomatoes
½ teaspoon dried oregano
50 g (2 oz) olives, pitted
salt and pepper to taste
TO SERVE:
grated Parmesan cheese*

1. First, prepare the sauce. Heat the oil in a pan, add the onion and red pepper and cook gently for 5 minutes, stirring occasionally. Add the remaining ingredients and cook for 5 minutes.
2. Cook the tagliatelle according to packet directions, drain well, then turn into a warmed serving dish.
3. Pour over the sauce and sprinkle with Parmesan cheese, or hand it separately, to serve.

Serves 4
Preparation time:
10 minutes
Cooking time:
10 minutes
Freezing:
Recommended for
sauce only

TOMATO AND EGG PLANT PANCAKES

1 large egg plant, diced
1 tablespoon olive oil
1 clove garlic, crushed
398 ml (14 oz) can
*   tomatoes*
1 tablespoon chopped
*   parsley*

12 Whole wheat Pancakes*
2 tablespoons grated
*   Parmesan cheese*
salt and pepper to taste
coriander sprigs to garnish

Serves 4–6
Preparation time:
20 minutes, plus
standing time and
making pancakes
Cooking time:
15 minutes
Freezing:
Recommended

1. Place the egg plant in a colander, sprinkle with salt and leave for 30 minutes. Rinse and dry with paper towels.
2. Heat the oil in a pan, add the egg plant and fry until golden, turning occasionally.
3. Add the garlic and fry for 1 minute, then add the tomatoes, parsley, and salt and pepper. Cover and simmer for 10 minutes, stirring occasionally.
4. Divide the filling between the pancakes, roll up and place in a lightly oiled, shallow ovenproof dish.
5. Sprinkle with the Parmesan cheese and bake in a preheated oven, 190°C/375°F, for 15 minutes, until heated through. Serve with a salad.

BEAN AND BACON FRITTATA

This recipe is Mexican in origin and is an excellent way of using left-over beans—any variety will do.

1 tablespoon oil
1 onion, chopped
1 celery stick, chopped
50 g (2 oz) slab bacon,
*   chopped*
4 eggs
2 tablespoons water

2 tablespoons chopped
*   parsley*
125 ml (1/2 cup) cooked
*   pinto beans*
salt and pepper to taste
oil for shallow-frying

Serves 2
Preparation time:
10 minutes, plus
cooking beans
Cooking time:
10–15 minutes
Freezing:
Not recommended

1. Heat the oil in a pan, add the onion, celery and bacon and fry for about 5 minutes, stirring.
2. Beat the eggs and water together in a bowl, then stir in the parsley, beans, onion mixture, and salt and pepper.
3. Heat the oil in a 23 cm (9 inch) frying pan, pour in the egg mixture and cook slowly for 4 minutes, until the frittata is beginning to set.
4. Remove from the heat and place under a preheated broiler for about 2 minutes, to finish cooking.
5. Slide onto a warmed serving dish and cut into wedges.

ZUCCHINI CRUMBLE

A good way to use up large zucchini.

2 tablespoons oil
2 onions, sliced
750 g (1½ lb) zucchini,
*   sliced*
2 cloves garlic, crushed
398 ml (14 oz) can
*   tomatoes*
1 teaspoon dried oregano
1 tablespoon tomato paste

salt and pepper to taste
FOR THE CRUMBLE:
300 ml (1¼ cups) whole
*   wheat flour*
2 tablespoons margarine
50 g (2 oz) Cheddar
*   cheese, grated finely*
25 g (1 oz) Parmesan
*   cheese, grated*

Serves 4
Preparation time:
35 minutes
Cooking time:
30 minutes
Freezing:
Not recommended

1. Heat the oil in a pan, add the onions and zucchini and fry for 10 minutes, stirring occasionally.
2. Add the garlic, tomatoes, oregano, tomato paste, and salt and pepper. Cover and simmer for 10 minutes, then turn into a 1.5 litre (6 cup) ovenproof dish.
3. To make the crumble, put the flour into a mixing bowl and rub in the margarine until the mixture resembles breadcrumbs. Stir in the cheeses.
4. Sprinkle the crumble over the zucchini mixture and bake in a preheated oven, 200°C/400°F, for 30 minutes, until golden brown.

SPINACH FLANS

*1 ¼ batches Whole wheat
    Pastry**
1 tablespoon oil
1 onion, chopped
2 cloves garlic, crushed
*500 g (1 lb) frozen
    chopped spinach,
    thawed*
4 tablespoons milk

2 eggs
*½ teaspoon grated
    nutmeg*
*175 g (6 oz) Ricotta or
    curd cheese*
*2 tablespoons grated
    Parmesan cheese*
1 tablespoon sesame seeds
salt and pepper to taste

1. Divide the pastry into 6 pieces. Roll out one piece on a floured surface and use to line a 10 cm (4 inch) fluted flan pan. Repeat with the remaining pastry. Chill in the refrigerator while making the filling.
2. Heat the oil in a pan, add the onion and fry until softened. Add the garlic and spinach and cook gently for 10 minutes, stirring occasionally.
3. Cool slightly, then beat in the milk, eggs, nutmeg, cheeses, and salt and pepper.
4. Divide the filling between the flan cases and sprinkle with the sesame seeds. Place on a baking sheet and bake in a preheated oven, 200°C/400°F, for 35–40 minutes, until firm. Serve warm or cold.

Serves 6
Preparation time:
20 minutes, plus
pastry making
Cooking time:
35–40 minutes
Freezing:
Recommended

MAIN COURSE DISHES

MINT FRICADELLES

Bulgur wheat is used as the base for these minty meat-balls. Serve with Tomato Sauce* and wholewheat pasta.

50 g (2 oz) bulgur wheat
250 g (8 oz) ground lamb
1 onion, chopped finely
1 clove garlic, crushed
2 tablespoons chopped
    mint
1 egg

2 teaspoons shoyu or soy
    sauce
3 tablespoons whole wheat
    flour
salt and pepper to taste
oil for shallow-frying

Serves 4
Preparation time:
15 minutes, plus
soaking time
Cooking time:
8 minutes
Freezing:
Recommended

1. Soak the bulgur wheat for 30 minutes; drain well. Wrap in a clean cloth and squeeze out all the moisture.
2. Place in a bowl with the remaining ingredients, except the flour, and mix together thoroughly.
3. Using dampened hands, shape the mixture into balls the size of a golf ball and roll in the flour.
4. Fry for about 8 minutes, turning occasionally. Drain on paper towels and serve immediately.

SHRIMP WITH ALMONDS

An attractive stir-fry dish that only takes minutes to cook. Serve with brown rice or Japanese egg noodles.

1 tablespoon sesame oil
1 onion, sliced
75 g (3 oz) split almonds
1 teaspoon chopped fresh
    ginger root
1 clove garlic, crushed
250 g (8 oz) fresh or
    frozen snow peas

350 g (12 oz) peeled
    shrimp
2 tablespoons dry sherry
1 tablespoon shoyu or soy
    sauce
2 tablespoons water
salt and pepper to taste

Serves 4
Preparation time:
8 minutes
Cooking time:
7 minutes
Freezing:
Not recommended

1. Heat the oil in a wok, add the onion and almonds and stir-fry over a high heat for 1 minute.
2. Add the ginger, garlic and snow peas and stir-fry for 2 minutes.
3. Add the remaining ingredients and stir-fry for 3 minutes, then serve immediately.

KEBABS WITH BULGUR PILAF

Bulgur wheat takes far less time to cook than other grains because it is cracked and partly cooked already, so it is very useful when you are in a rush.

KEBABS:
1 tablespoon olive oil
2 tablespoons lemon juice
1 tablespoon shoyu or soy sauce
1 clove garlic, crushed
1 teaspoon chopped rosemary
500 g (1 lb) lean lamb, boned and cut into 2.5 cm (1 inch) cubes
1 large red pepper, cored, seeded and cut into 2.5 cm (1 inch) squares

3 small onions, each cut into 8 pieces
BULGUR PILAF:
175 g (6 oz) bulgur wheat
1 tablespoon oil
1 onion, chopped
1 red pepper, cored, seeded and diced
125 g (4 oz) mushrooms, sliced
1 tablespoon chopped parsley
1 tablespoon shoyu or soy sauce

Serves 4
Preparation time:
15 minutes, plus marinating
Cooking time:
20 minutes
Freezing:
Not recommended

1. For the kebabs, mix together the oil, lemon juice, shoyu or soy sauce, garlic and rosemary, pour over the meat and leave to marinate for 2 hours, turning occasionally.
2. Thread alternate pieces of lamb, red pepper and onion onto 8 skewers, then baste with the marinade.
3. Cook under a preheated broiler for 8 minutes, turning and basting frequently.
4. For the pilaf, cook the bulgur wheat in boiling salted water for 10 minutes, or until tender; drain well.
5. Heat the oil in a pan, add the onion and red pepper and fry for 5 minutes. Add the mushrooms and cook for 2 minutes, stirring.
6. Stir in the bulgur wheat, parsley and shoyu or soy sauce. Turn into a serving dish and arrange the kebabs on top.

RUSSIAN FISH PIE

1 tablespoon oil
1 onion, chopped
125 g (4 oz) mushrooms, sliced
50 ml (¼ cup) brown rice, cooked
2 tablespoons chopped parsley

350 g (12 oz) Finnan haddock, cooked and flaked
1½ batches Whole wheat Pastry*
salt and pepper to taste
beaten egg to glaze

1. Heat the oil in a pan, add the onion and fry until softened. Add the mushrooms and fry, stirring, for 3–4 minutes.

2. Add to the rice with the parsley, haddock, and salt and pepper.

3. Divide the pastry in half and roll out one piece to form a rectangle 30 × 18 cm (12 × 7 inches).

4. Place on a baking sheet and cover with the filling, leaving a 2.5 cm (1 inch) border all the way round; dampen these edges.

5. Roll out the remaining pastry slightly larger than the first piece. Cover the filling and trim the edges to fit. Press together, pinch the edges to seal and make 2 holes in the top. Decorate with leaves cut from the trimmings.

6. Brush with beaten egg and bake in a preheated oven, 200°C/400°F, for 30 minutes, until golden. Serve with Watercress Sauce*.

Serves 4–6
Preparation time: 30 minutes, plus pastry making, and cooking rice and fish
Cooking time: 30 minutes
Freezing: Recommended

TOMATO AND NUT CANNELLONI

This cannelloni has a rich nutty filling which blends well with the creamy sauce. The filling also makes a good sauce to go with wholewheat tagliatelle if you add a little stock or tomato juice to thin it down.

8 sheets dried wholewheat lasagne
FOR THE FILLING:
1 tablespoon sunflower oil
1 onion, chopped
1 celery stick, chopped
1 tablespoon whole wheat flour
1 clove garlic, crushed
398 ml (14 oz) can tomatoes
125 g (4 oz) mushrooms, sliced
1 tablespoon tomato paste
1 teaspoon soy sauce
1/2 teaspoon dried oregano

75 g (3 oz) hazelnuts, chopped finely
2 tablespoons chopped parsley
salt and pepper to taste
FOR THE SAUCE:
2 tablespoons sunflower oil
2 tablespoons whole wheat flour
300 ml (1 1/4 cups) milk
pinch of grated nutmeg
2 tablespoons grated Parmesan cheese
TO GARNISH:
sage or parsley sprigs

Serves 4
Preparation time:
35 minutes
Cooking time:
15–20 minutes
Freezing:
Recommended, at end of stage 6

1. Cook the pasta according to packet instructions. Drain, spread on paper towels and pat dry.
2. For the filling, heat the oil in a pan, add the onion and celery and fry gently until softened.
3. Stir in the flour, then add the garlic, tomatoes, mushrooms, tomato paste, soy sauce, oregano, and salt and pepper.
4. Bring to the boil, lower the heat and simmer for 8–10 minutes. Stir in the hazelnuts and parsley.
5. Spread a rounded tablespoon of filling over each piece of pasta. Roll up loosely from the shorter side and place join side down in a greased ovenproof dish.
6. For the sauce, heat the oil in a pan, then stir in the flour. Remove from the heat and stir in the milk. Bring to the boil, stirring constantly, then add the nutmeg, and salt and pepper. Pour over the pasta and sprinkle with the cheese.
7. Bake in a preheated oven, 200°C/400°F, for 15–20 minutes, until golden. Garnish with sage or parsley sprigs to serve.

VARIATION
Use ground walnuts or almonds in place of the hazelnuts. Chopped coriander can be used instead of the parsley.

BEANBURGERS

You can use any beans for this recipe. Serve with Coriander and Yogurt Sauce*, a salad and crusty bread.

*250 ml (1 cup) black eye
    beans, cooked*
3 tablespoons oil
1 onion, chopped
1 celery stick, chopped
2 cloves garlic, crushed
1 teaspoon turmeric

*2 teaspoons ground
    coriander*
*2 tablespoons tomato
    paste*
*50 ml (¼ cup) whole wheat
    breadcrumbs*
salt and pepper to taste

1. Purée the beans in a food processor.
2. Heat 1 tablespoon of the oil in a pan, add the onion and
celery and fry until softened. Add the garlic and spices and
fry for 1 minute.
3. Mix the beans with the fried vegetables and tomato
paste, then season with salt and pepper.
4. Shape into 8 burgers and coat with the breadcrumbs.
5. Heat the remaining oil in a pan, add the burgers and fry
for 3 minutes on each side, until golden.

Serves 4
Preparation time:
25 minutes, plus
cooking beans
Cooking time:
6 minutes
Freezing:
Recommended

CHICK PEA CASSEROLE

If you sprinkle the diced egg plant with salt and leave for 30 minutes, it removes the bitter juices and reduces the amount of oil needed for frying. Serve with brown rice.

375 ml (1½ cups) chick peas cooked
1 egg plant, diced
1 tablespoon olive oil
2 cloves garlic, crushed
1 teaspoon ground cumin

398 ml (14 oz) can tomatoes
2 tablespoons tomato paste
2 tablespoons chopped coriander leaves
salt and pepper to taste

Serves 4
Preparation time: 15 minutes, plus standing time and cooking chick peas
Cooking time: 30 minutes
Freezing: Recommended

1. Drain the chick peas, reserving 300 ml (1¼ cups) of the liquid, and set aside.
2. Place the diced egg plant in a colander, sprinkle with salt and leave for 30 minutes. Rinse well and pat dry with paper towels.
3. Heat the oil in a pan, add the egg plant and fry until golden, turning occasionally. Add the garlic and cumin, fry for 1 minute, then add the tomatoes with their juice, tomato paste, coriander, chick peas and reserved liquid.
4. Season with salt and pepper, bring to the boil, cover and simmer for 30 minutes. Serve in a shallow dish.

BLACK BEAN HOT POT

This is an adaptable recipe, suitable for all types of beans. I like it with Endive and Avocado Salad (page 44).

375 ml (1½ cups) black beans, cooked
2 tablespoons oil
2 onions, sliced
2 carrots, sliced
2 celery sticks, sliced
4 cloves garlic, crushed
1 tablespoon tomato paste

398 ml (14 oz) can tomatoes
2 tablespoons shoyu or soy sauce
1 tablespoon chopped parsley
75 g (3 oz) old Cheddar cheese, grated

1. Drain the beans, reserving 300 ml (1¼ cups) of the liquid, and set aside.
2. Heat the oil in a pan, add the onion and fry until softened. Add the carrot, celery and garlic and fry for 5 minutes, stirring occasionally.
3. Add the reserved bean liquid, beans, tomato paste, tomatoes with their juice and shoyu or soy sauce. Cover and simmer for 45 minutes.
4. Stir in the parsley, then turn into a shallow ovenproof dish and sprinkle with the cheese.
5. Place under a preheated broiler, until golden.

Serves 4
Preparation time: 20 minutes, plus cooking beans
Cooking time: 50 minutes
Freezing: Recommended, at end of stage 4

CURRIED CHICK PEA RISSOLES

These spicy rissoles are delicious served with Bulgur Pilaf (see page 34) and Coriander and Yogurt Sauce*.

4 tablespoons sunflower oil
1 onion, chopped
1 celery stick, chopped
1 clove garlic, crushed
½ teaspoon turmeric
1 teaspoon ground cumin
1 teaspoon garam masala
175 ml (¾ cup) red lentils
450 ml (1¾ cups) water

250 ml (1 cup) cooked chick peas
125 ml (½ cup) whole wheat breadcrumbs
1 tablespoon chopped coriander leaves
4 tablespoons whole wheat flour
salt and pepper to taste
celery leaves to garnish

Serves 4
Preparation time:
40 minutes, plus cooking chick peas
Cooking time:
6 minutes
Freezing:
Recommended

1. Heat 1 tablespoon of the oil in a pan, add the onion and celery and cook until softened.
2. Add the garlic and spices and cook for 1 minute, stirring constantly.
3. Add the lentils and water, bring to the boil, cover and simmer for 20 minutes, stirring occasionally.
4. Remove from the heat and mix in the chick peas, breadcrumbs, coriander, and salt and pepper. Leave to cool slightly.
5. Using dampened hands, shape the mixture into small balls, then flatten slightly and roll in the flour.
6. Heat the remaining oil in a large frying pan, add the rissoles and fry for 3 minutes on each side, until crisp and golden. Drain on paper towels and serve immediately, garnished with celery leaves.

CASHEW NUT LOAF

Nut loaves can be dry; this one is really tasty and moist.

1 tablespoon oil
1 onion, chopped
1 celery stick, chopped
1 clove garlic, crushed
50 g (2 oz) mushrooms, chopped
1 tablespoon whole wheat flour
398 ml (14 oz) can tomatoes

125 g (4 oz) cashew nuts, ground
250 ml (1 cup) whole wheat breadcrumbs
1 tablespoon shoyu or soy sauce
2 tablespoons chopped parsley
1 egg
salt and pepper to taste

1. Grease and line a 1.5 L (8 × 4 inch) loaf pan.
2. Heat the oil in a pan, add the onion and celery and fry until softened.
3. Add the garlic and mushrooms and fry for 3 minutes, stirring occasionally.
4. Mix in the flour, then add the tomatoes and cook until thickened.
5. Add the remaining ingredients and mix together thoroughly.
6. Turn into the prepared pan, cover with foil and cook in a preheated oven, 180°C/350°F, for 1 hour.
7. Turn out onto a warmed serving dish. Serve in slices with Tomato Sauce* handed separately.

Serves 4
Preparation time:
15 minutes
Cooking time:
1 hour
Freezing:
Recommended

VARIATION
Replace the cashews with walnuts or hazelnuts.

SHRIMP PILAF

This dish is also very good made with monk fish – replace the shrimp with cooked cubed fish. Almonds make a good alternative to cashew nuts.

2 tablespoons oil
1 onion, chopped
2 celery sticks, sliced
250 ml (1 cup) brown rice
600 ml (2½ cups) water (approximately)
1 red pepper, cored, seeded and diced

50 g (2 oz) cashew nuts
1 clove garlic, crushed
125 g (4 oz) button mushrooms, sliced
350 g (12 oz) peeled shrimp
2 tablespoons chopped dill
salt and pepper to taste

Serves 4
Preparation time:
15 minutes
Cooking time:
40–45 minutes
Freezing:
Not recommended

1. Heat 1 tablespoon of the oil in a pan, add the onion and celery and fry until softened.
2. Add the rice and cook for 2 minutes, stirring to coat it in the oil. Add the water and 1 teaspoon salt and bring to the boil.
3. Cover and simmer for 35–40 minutes, adding more water if necessary.
4. Meanwhile, heat the remaining oil in a pan, add the red pepper and cashew nuts and fry for 3 minutes, stirring occasionally.
5. Add the garlic and mushrooms and fry for 3 minutes, stirring occasionally.
6. Add to the rice with the shrimp, dill, and salt and pepper and heat through. Serve immediately.

BEAN AND MUSHROOM AU GRATIN

You need a soft textured bean for this recipe, to absorb the full flavour of mushrooms and garlic. I like it best with melted Mozzarella cheese on top, but use another cheese suitable for melting if you prefer.

250 ml (1 cup) butter beans, cooked
2 tablespoons skim milk powder
1 tablespoon oil
1 onion, chopped
350 g (12 oz) mushrooms, sliced
2 cloves garlic, crushed

2 tablespoons whole wheat flour
2 tablespoons chopped parsley
175 g (6 oz) Mozzarella cheese, sliced
salt and pepper to taste
coriander leaves to garnish

1. Drain the beans, reserving 300 ml (1¼ cups) of the liquid, and set aside.
2. Stir the milk powder into the reserved liquid.
3. Heat the oil in a pan, add the onion and fry until softened.
4. Add the mushrooms and garlic and fry gently for 2 minutes, stirring occasionally.
5. Stir in the flour, then pour in the milky bean liquid and cook, stirring, until thickened. Add the parsley, beans, and salt and pepper.
6. Turn into a shallow ovenproof dish and lay the cheese slices over the top. Cook under a preheated broiler for 3–4 minutes, until the cheese has melted.
7. Garnish with coriander to serve.

Serves 4
Preparation time: 15 minutes, plus cooking beans
Cooking time: 10 minutes
Freezing: Recommended, at end of stage 6

WATERMELON VINAIGRETTE

A colourful and unusual salad that delights everyone who tries it. It also makes a refreshing starter.

500 g (1 lb) watermelon
125 g (4 oz) bean sprouts
2 tablespoons sesame seeds, toasted

1 bunch watercress
2 teaspoons lemon juice
2 tablespoons olive oil
salt and pepper to taste

Serves 4
Preparation time:
15 minutes
Freezing:
Not recommended

1. Pick out the seeds from the watermelon and discard. Cut the flesh from the skin, then slice it diagonally into wedges.
2. Place in a serving bowl with the bean sprouts, sesame seeds and watercress.
3. Mix the lemon juice, oil, and salt and pepper together and pour over the salad. Toss thoroughly before serving.

ENDIVE AND AVOCADO SALAD

A green salad with a difference. Curly endive looks really pretty in a salad and has a slightly bitter flavour that combines well with the soft texture of the avocado and the nutty flavour of the sesame seeds.

1 small curly endive
1 bunch watercress
1 avocado, halved and stoned

6 tablespoons Herb Vinaigrette*
1 tablespoon sesame seeds, toasted

Serves 6–8
Preparation time:
20 minutes, plus making dressing
Freezing:
Not recommended

1. Tear the endive into pieces and separate the watercress into sprigs. Place in a salad bowl.
2. Peel the avocado and slice into a bowl. Pour over the dressing and toss until well coated.
3. Add to the endive and watercress with the sesame seeds and toss thoroughly.

PINTO BEAN SALAD

You can use any of the larger beans for this salad, but pinto beans have a particularly nice soft texture and take less time to cook than most.

175 ml (¾ cup) pinto beans, cooked
3 green onions, sliced thinly
75 g (3 oz) bean sprouts
2 tomatoes, chopped
2 celery sticks, chopped
2 tablespoons chopped parsley
3 tablespoons Shoyu Dressing*

Serves 4
Preparation time: 10 minutes, plus cooking beans and making dressing
Freezing: Not recommended

1. Place all the ingredients in a mixing bowl and toss thoroughly. Turn into a shallow serving dish.

FENNEL AND CRESS SALAD

This fresh and tangy salad goes well with fish dishes.

2 bulbs fennel
2 tablespoons lemon juice
2 tablespoons olive oil
2 cartons mustard and cress
salt and pepper to taste

Serves 4
Preparation time: 15 minutes, plus marinating
Freezing: Not recommended

1. Trim the stalks, base and outer leaves from the fennel.
2. Cut the bulbs in half and shred finely. Place in a salad bowl with the lemon juice, oil, and salt and pepper. Toss thoroughly and leave to marinate for 2 hours.
3. Add the cress and toss again before serving.

SPROUTED MUNG SALAD

If you sprout mung beans at home you can use them at varying stages. If you use them when still quite short, they have a nutty flavour.

175 g (6 oz) sprouted mung beans
2 tomatoes, chopped
2 tablespoons chopped parsley
2 celery sticks, chopped
6 green onions, sliced thinly
4 tablespoons Shoyu Dressing*

Serves 4
Preparation time: 10 minutes, plus making dressing
Freezing: Not recommended

1. Place the sprouted beans in a salad bowl with the tomato, parsley, celery and green onions.
2. Pour over the dressing and toss thoroughly.

CAULIFLOWER SALAD

Very lightly blanched cauliflower with celery and a Stilton dressing makes a happy combination. If you want a more substantial salad, add some crumbly Wensleydale cheese.

*1 small cauliflower,
    broken into florets
2 celery sticks, sliced thinly
50 g (2 oz) blue Stilton
    cheese*

*125 ml (½ cup) yogurt
2 tablespoons chopped
    parsley
salt and pepper to taste*

**Serves 6
Preparation time:**
15 minutes
Freezing:
Not recommended

1. Blanch the cauliflower in boiling salted water for 2 minutes. Drain and place in a mixing bowl with the celery.
2. Mash the cheese with a fork and gradually add the yogurt to make a smooth paste, seasoning with salt and pepper.
3. Pour over the cauliflower, add the parsley and mix until completely coated. Transfer to a serving bowl.

CURRIED POTATO SALAD

A lovely combination of egg and potato with a lightly curried creamy sauce.

*750 g (1½ lb) new
    potatoes
2 tablespoons French
    Dressing*
6 green onions, sliced
    thinly
150 ml (⅔ cup) yogurt*

*2 teaspoons tomato paste
1 teaspoon concentrated
    curry paste
2 hard-boiled eggs, cut into
    8 wedges
salt to taste*

**Serves 6
Preparation time:**
35 minutes, plus
making dressing
Freezing:
Not recommended

1. Cook the potatoes in their skins in boiling salted water for about 20 minutes, until tender. Drain well, cut into chunks and place in a bowl with the French dressing and green onions.
2. Mix together the yogurt, tomato paste and curry paste until smooth.
3. Pour over the potatoes, add the eggs and mix well until coated. Transfer to a serving dish.

RICE AND ALMOND SALAD

A filling salad, particularly useful to serve at buffet parties. The choice of vegetables you can use is endless—vary according to what is in season.

175 ml (¾ cup) brown rice, cooked
6 green onions, chopped
1 red pepper, cored, seeded and chopped
50 g (2 oz) raisins
50 g (2 oz) split almonds, browned
2 celery sticks, chopped
175 ml (¾ cup) cooked kernel corn
2 tablespoons chopped parsley
6 tablespoons French Dressing*

Serves 8
Preparation time: 15 minutes, plus cooking rice and kernel corn and making dressing
Freezing: Not recommended

1. Place all the ingredients in a bowl and toss thoroughly. Transfer to a serving dish.

RED CABBAGE WITH APPLE

A very colourful winter vegetable accompaniment with a sweet and sour flavour. Ideal to serve with game or any rich meat.

500 g (1 lb) red cabbage
1 tablespoon oil
1 onion, sliced thinly
1 eating apple, cored and
  sliced thinly
1–2 teaspoons liquid honey

2 tablespoons cider
  vinegar
2 tablespoons chopped
  parsley
salt and pepper to taste

Serves 4
Preparation time:
20 minutes
Cooking time:
20–30 minutes
Freezing:
Recommended

1. Quarter the cabbage and shred finely, discarding the stalk. Place in a large pan of fast boiling water and blanch for 3 minutes. Drain, reserving the liquid.
2. Heat the oil in a flameproof casserole, add the onion and fry until softened. Add the apple, stir, cover and cook for 3 minutes.
3. Add the honey, vinegar, 2 tablespoons of the reserved liquid, cabbage, and salt and pepper. Stir thoroughly to mix.
4. Cover and cook in a preheated oven, 180°C/350°F, for 20–30 minutes, stirring once or twice.
5. Stir in the parsley, transfer to a warmed serving dish and serve immediately.

DAHL

Dahl is a quickly made accompaniment to serve with a curry. You can use green or brown lentils for a change, but the consistency will not be so smooth.

1 tablespoon oil
1 onion, chopped
2 cloves garlic, crushed
2 teaspoons ground
  coriander
1 teaspoon cumin seeds

1 teaspoon turmeric
175 ml (3/4 cup) red lentils
600 ml (2 1/2 cups) water
1 tablespoon chopped
  coriander leaves
salt and pepper to taste

Serves 4
Preparation time:
10 minutes
Cooking time:
20 minutes
Freezing:
Recommended

1. Heat the oil in a pan, add the onion and cook until softened. Add the garlic and spices and fry for 1 minute.
2. Add the lentils and water and bring to the boil. Cover and simmer for 20 minutes, stirring occasionally.
3. Add the coriander, salt and pepper, and a little more water if necessary. Transfer to a warmed serving dish.

STIR-FRIED BEAN SPROUTS

This dish makes a lovely accompaniment to barbecued spare ribs. It can be easily varied according to the vegetables you have to hand.

1 tablespoon sesame oil
1 large onion, sliced
2 celery sticks, sliced
2 cloves garlic, crushed
1 red pepper, cored, seeded and sliced
175 g (6 oz) fresh or frozen snow peas
175 g (6 oz) button mushrooms, sliced

500 g (1 lb) bean sprouts
2 tablespoons shoyu or soy sauce
2 tablespoons dry sherry
½ teaspoon 5-spice powder (optional)
1 tablespoon chopped parsley
salt and pepper to taste

Serves 4
Preparation time:
15 minutes
Cooking time:
6 minutes
Freezing:
Not recommended

1. Heat the oil in a wok, add the onion and celery and stir-fry for 2 minutes.
2. Add the garlic, red pepper and snow peas and stir-fry for 2 minutes.
3. Add the remaining ingredients and stir-fry for 2 minutes, until heated through.

JULIENNE OF VEGETABLES

An easy way to make the more mundane root vegetables into a really wonderful dish – ideal to serve at a dinner party in the autumn or winter.

1 onion
1 leek
2 celery sticks
2 carrots
1 tablespoon sunflower oil

4 tablespoons water
2 tablespoons chopped
parsley
salt and pepper to taste

1. Slice the onion thickly and separate into rings, then cut into strips.
2. Cut the remaining vegetables into thin strips, about 5 cm (2 inches) in length.
3. Heat the oil in a large heavy-based pan, add the onion and cook until softened.
4. Add the remaining vegetables and stir-fry for about 5 minutes.
5. Add the water, and salt and pepper, cover and simmer for about 5 minutes.
6. Stir in the parsley and turn into a warmed serving dish.

Serves 4
Preparation time:
30 minutes
Cooking time:
15 minutes
Freezing:
Recommended

POTATOES IN GARLIC SAUCE

Choose small new potatoes and don't peel them: the skin provides extra fibre as well as more flavour.

500 g (1 lb) new potatoes
175 g (6 oz) button
  mushrooms
1 tablespoon olive oil
1 clove garlic, crushed
1 tablespoon whole wheat
  flour

150 ml (²/₃ cup) skim
  milk
pinch of grated nutmeg
2 tablespoons snipped
  chives
salt and pepper to taste

Serves 4
Preparation time:
10 minutes
Cooking time:
20 minutes
Freezing:
Not recommended

1. Cook the potatoes in boiling salted water for 15 minutes, until just tender. Drain and set aside.
2. Wipe the mushrooms and trim the stalks level with the caps.
3. Heat the oil in a pan, add the mushrooms and garlic and fry for 1 minute.
4. Mix in the flour, then stir in the milk. Season with nutmeg, salt and pepper. Bring to the boil, stirring, and cook for 3 minutes, until thickened.
5. Add the potatoes and chives, cover and heat through for a few minutes.

POMMES SAVOYARDE

A potato dish that's full of flavour—with the addition of a little smoked ham it makes a good lunch dish.

750 g (1¹/₂ lb) potatoes
  (not peeled)
1 clove garlic, chopped
  finely

75 g (3 oz) Gruyère cheese,
  grated
300 ml (1¹/₄ cups) milk
salt and pepper to taste

Serves 6
Preparation time:
20 minutes
Cooking time:
1¹/₂ hours
Freezing:
Not recommended

1. Slice the potatoes thinly and arrange half in a layer in a greased, large, shallow, ovenproof dish. Sprinkle with the garlic, half the cheese, and salt and pepper. Cover with the remaining potatoes.
2. Pour in enough milk to come almost level with the top of the potatoes, then sprinkle with the remaining cheese.
3. Cook in a preheated oven, 200°C/400°F, for about 1¹/₂ hours, until the potatoes are soft and golden.

BRUSSELS SPROUT PURÉE

A vegetable accompaniment with an intriguing flavour.
Prepare when you can only get large sprouts.

*350 g (12 oz) Brussels
    sprouts
50 ml (¼ cup) whole wheat
    breadcrumbs
2 teaspoons lemon juice*

*125 g (4 oz) Ricotta
    cheese
½ teaspoon grated
    nutmeg
salt and pepper to taste*

1. Cook the sprouts in boiling salted water for about 10 minutes; drain, reserving the liquid.
2. Place in a food processor or blender with the remaining ingredients and work until smooth, adding a little of the cooking liquid if necessary. Return to the pan to heat through, check the seasoning and serve.

Serves 4
Preparation time:
10 minutes
Cooking time:
10 minutes
Freezing:
Not recommended

DESSERTS

APRICOT FOOL

It is preferable to boil dried apricots in water to cover for
1 minute, then drain, to clean the fruit before using.

125 g (4 oz) dried apricots　　*300 ml (1¼ cups) yogurt*
250 ml (1 cup) orange　　　　*4 tablespoons thick*
*　juice*　　　　　　　　　　*　yogurt*

Serves 6
Preparation time:
15 minutes
Cooking time:
20 minutes
Freezing:
Not recommended

1. Place the apricots and orange juice in a pan, bring to the
boil, cover and simmer for 20 minutes. Allow to cool.
2. Purée in a food processor or blender.
3. Mix the yogurt until smooth, then fold in all but
1 tablespoon of the apricot purée.
4. Spoon into individual dishes. Swirl a spoonful of
thick yogurt on top of each one, then swirl in the remaining apricot purée.

SUMMER PEACHES

A delicious combination of peaches, strawberries and
raspberries. I often serve this in the strawberry season as
it's so quick to prepare. It can be served without the
addition of the liqueur, but this does impart a particularly
good flavour!

50 g (2 oz) raspberries　　　*2 peaches, peeled and*
2 tablespoons liqueur de　　*　pitted*
*　Framboise or Cointreau*　　*175 g (6 oz) strawberries,*
*　　　　　　　　　　　　　　sliced*

Serves 4
Preparation time:
15 minutes
Freezing:
Not recommended

1. Sieve the raspberries into a bowl, then stir in the
liqueur.
2. Slice the peaches into the raspberry purée. Add the
strawberries and turn gently to coat the fruit completely.
3. Chill until required. Serve with yogurt.

ORANGE CHARTREUSE

A refreshing dessert, easy to prepare and ideal to serve at a dinner party as it looks so attractive.

4 oranges
300 ml (1¼ cups) apple juice
2 teaspoons gelatine

2 tablespoons Cointreau
125 g (4 oz) strawberries
1 tablespoon liquid honey
strawberry leaves (optional)

Serves 6
Preparation time: 30 minutes
Setting time: 2 hours
Freezing: Not recommended

1. Peel and segment the oranges, discarding all the pith and pips. Divide the orange segments and any juice between 6 small ramekins or individual moulds.
2. Put half the apple juice in a small pan, sprinkle over the gelatine and leave to soak for 5 minutes.
3. Heat gently until dissolved, then add the remaining apple juice and the Cointreau. Pour over the oranges and leave in the refrigerator until set.
4. Purée the strawberries in a blender or food processor and mix with the honey. Spoon a little strawberry purée onto each serving plate.
5. Dip the ramekins or moulds quickly in hot water, then invert each dessert onto the strawberry purée.
6. Decorate with strawberry leaves, if you have any.

APRICOT YOGURT ICE

A very easy ice cream to make, using set yogurt instead of cream. It can also be made, very successfully, with other dried fruits; I especially like it with prunes.

*250 g (8 oz) dried apricots,
soaked for 2 hours
350 ml (1¾ cups) apple
juice
2 egg whites*

*2 tablespoons liquid honey
250 ml (1 cup) thick yogurt
sliced strawberries to
decorate*

1. Place the apricots and apple juice in a pan, cover and cook gently for 20 minutes.
2. Cool slightly, then purée in a food processor or blender. Leave to cool completely.
3. Whisk the egg whites until stiff, then gradually whisk in the honey.
4. Beat the yogurt until smooth, then fold into the apricot purée. Fold in the egg white mixture.
5. Turn into a rigid freezerproof container, cover, seal and freeze until solid.
6. Transfer to the refrigerator 40 minutes before serving, to soften. Scoop into individual dishes and decorate with sliced strawberries to serve.

Serves 6
Preparation time:
15 minutes, plus soaking time
Cooking time:
20 minutes
Freezing time:
4 hours

PEAR MOUSSE

A simple mousse with a stronger flavour than you can achieve with fresh pears.

125 g (4 oz) dried pears,
*   soaked overnight*
125 ml (½ cup) curd
*   cheese*
1 tablespoon lemon juice

1 egg white
1 tablespoon liquid honey
1 pear, sliced thinly, to
*   decorate*

Serves 4
Preparation time:
15 minutes, plus
soaking time
Cooking time:
30 minutes
Freezing:
Not recommended

1. Cook the pears in 450 ml (1¾ cups) of the soaking liquid for 30 minutes. Drain, reserving 2 tablespoons liquid..
2. Cool, then place the pears and reserved liquid in a food processor or blender with the cheese and 2 teaspoons of the lemon juice and work until smooth.
3. Whisk the egg white until stiff, then whisk in the honey.
4. Fold the egg white into the pear mixture, then spoon into individual glasses. Decorate with pear slices, brushed with the remaining lemon juice, to serve.

VARIATION
Prune Mousse: Use 125 g (4 oz) pitted prunes instead of the dried pears and cook for 15 minutes only. Use 1 tablespoon chopped nuts to decorate the mousse.

PARADISE PUDDING

As you'll guess from the name, this is one of my favourites. When strawberries are not in season, use other fresh fruits. The oatmeal gives a lovely chewy texture and added fibre.

125 ml (½ cup) almonds
*   chopped finely*
125 ml (½ cup) fine oatmeal
1 tablespoon liquid honey
1 tablespoon Cointreau

250 ml (1 cup) thick
*   yogurt*
175 g (6 oz) strawberries,
*   sliced*

Serves 4
Preparation time:
15 minutes
Freezing:
Not recommended

1. Place the almonds and oatmeal under a preheated broiler, turning frequently, until brown; cool.
2. Mix the honey and Cointreau together, fold into the yogurt, then fold in the almond mixture.
3. Divide the strawberries between 4 glasses, reserving a few slices for decoration.
4. Spoon the oat cream over the strawberries and decorate with the reserved strawberry slices.

· APPLE JALOUSIE

Use eating apples rather than cookers, so that extra sugar is unnecessary. The dates and spices also add natural sweetness to the dessert.

500 g (1 lb) eating apples,
*   cored and chopped*
125 g (4 oz) chopped dates
1 teaspoon ground mixed
*   spice*

370 g (13 oz) packet
*   whole wheat puff pastry*
beaten egg to glaze
1 tablespoon sesame seeds

Serves 4
Preparation time:
25 minutes
Cooking time:
20–25 minutes
Freezing:
Recommended

1. Place the apples, dates and spice in a mixing bowl and mix thoroughly.
2. Cut the pastry in half and roll out one piece on a lightly floured surface to a rectangle measuring 30 × 23 cm (12 × 9 inches).
3. Place on a baking sheet and spread the apple mixture over the pastry to within 2.5 cm (1 inch) of the edges. Dampen the edges with water.
4. Roll out the remaining pastry to a rectangle slightly larger than the first. Flour the pastry lightly and fold in half lengthways.
5. Cut through the folded edge of the pastry at 1 cm (½ inch) intervals to within 2.5 cm (1 inch) of the edges.
6. Unfold and place over the apple. Seal the pastry edges, then knock up with the back of a knife.
7. Brush with beaten egg and sprinkle with the sesame seeds. Bake in a preheated oven, 200°C/400°F, for 20–25 minutes, until golden.
8. Serve warm or cold.

STRAWBERRY NUT SPONGE

A luscious strawberry cake which is equally good eaten as a dessert or at teatime. A great favourite with my children and their friends.

2 eggs
3 tablespoons liquid honey
½ teaspoon ground
*   cinnamon, sifted*
125 ml (½ cup) whole wheat
*   flour*
25 g (1 oz) ground
*   almonds*

1 tablespoon chopped
*   almonds*
175 ml (¾ cup) yogurt
*   with strawberries*
125 g (4 oz) strawberries,
*   sliced*

1. Grease and line a 20 cm (8 inch) cake pan.
2. Whisk the eggs and honey together until thick and mousse-like, using an electric whisk.
3. Carefully fold in the cinnamon, flour and ground almonds, using a metal spoon. Turn into the prepared pan and sprinkle with the chopped almonds.
4. Bake in a preheated oven, 190°C/375°F, for 18–20 minutes, until the cake springs back when lightly pressed.
5. Carefully remove the cake from the pan and cool on a wire rack.
6. Split the cake in half horizontally and sandwich together with the yogurt and sliced strawberries.

Serves 6
Preparation time: 15 minutes
Cooking time: 18–20 minutes
Freezing: Recommended, at end of stage 6

LEBANESE FRUIT SALAD

An attractive dessert which is delicious on its own or served with yogurt. Any left over is very good served with Granola (page 10) for breakfast.

125 g (4 oz) dried apricots
125 g (4 oz) pitted prunes
450 ml (1¾ cups) apple juice
1 large orange

125 g (4 oz) fresh dates, halved and pitted
1 tablespoon pumpkin seeds
2 tablespoons pine nuts

Serves 4
Preparation time: 15 minutes
Cooking time: 15 minutes
Freezing: Recommended, at end of stage 2

1. Place the apricots, prunes and apple juice in a pan and bring to the boil. Cover and simmer for 15 minutes. Leave to cool, with the lid on the pan.
2. Peel the orange and divide into segments, discarding all pith and pips. Add the orange segments and dates to the other fruit and toss gently. Divide between individual serving dishes and chill until required.
3. Put the seeds and nuts in a heavy-based pan and place over a high heat, shaking the pan constantly, until they begin to pop and brown.
4. Sprinkle over the fruit and serve immediately.

PRUNE AND CHEESE PANCAKES

This dessert is also very good made with dried apricots, or with stewed apples and raisins. They are all quite sweet enough to make the addition of sugar unnecessary.

250 g (8 oz) pitted prunes, chopped
300 ml (1¼ cups) apple juice
12 Whole wheat Pancakes*

175 g (6 oz) Ricotta cheese
1 tablespoon liquid honey
2 tablespoons sliced almonds, browned

Serves 4
Preparation time: 5 minutes, plus pancake making
Cooking time: 25 minutes
Freezing: Recommended, at end of stage 2

1. Place the prunes and apple juice in a pan, cover and simmer for 15 minutes, stirring occasionally, until the liquid has been absorbed.
2. Place a little of the prune mixture on each pancake, then top with a spoonful of Ricotta cheese. Roll up and arrange in an ovenproof dish.
3. Warm the honey and brush over the pancakes to glaze. Place in a preheated oven, 180°C/350°F, for about 10 minutes, to heat through. Sprinkle with the almonds to serve.

BAKING

DATE AND ORANGE TEABREAD

250 ml (1 cup) All-Bran
125 g (4 oz) dried chopped
   dates
300 ml (1¼ cups) orange
   juice
1 tablespoon liquid honey

50 g (2 oz) sunflower seeds
250 ml (1 cup) whole
   wheat flour
2 teaspoons baking
   powder

**Makes one 1.5 L
(8 × 4 inch) loaf
Preparation time:**
15 minutes, plus
soaking time
Cooking time:
55–60 minutes
Freezing:
Recommended

1. Grease and line a 1.5 L (8 × 4 inch) loaf pan.
2. Put the Bran, dates, orange juice and honey in a mixing bowl. Stir well and leave for 1 hour.
3. Add the sunflower seeds and flour, then sift in the baking powder and mix together thoroughly.
4. Turn into the prepared pan and bake in a preheated oven, 180°C/350°F, for 55–60 minutes, or until a skewer inserted into the centre comes out clean.
5. Turn onto a wire rack to cool.

SPICED APPLE SCONES

Use soft margarine to avoid the rubbing-in process. Don't
peel the apples—it adds extra fibre.

500 ml (2 cups) whole wheat
   flour
1 teaspoon cream of
   tartar, sifted
½ teaspoon baking
   soda, sifted
1 teaspoon ground
   cinnamon, sifted

50 g (2 oz) soft margarine
1 eating apple, cored and
   grated
6 tablespoons milk
1 tablespoon liquid honey
milk and sesame seeds
   to glaze

**Makes 12
Preparation time:**
15 minutes
Cooking time:
12–15 minutes
Freezing:
Recommended

1. Place all the ingredients in a bowl and mix with a fork to form a soft dough.
2. Turn onto a well floured surface, knead lightly and roll out to a 2 cm (¾ inch) thickness.
3. Cut into 5 cm (2 inch) rounds with a fluted cutter.
4. Place on a floured baking sheet, brush with milk and sprinkle with sesame seeds. Bake in a preheated oven, 220°C/425°F, for 12–15 minutes. Transfer to a wire rack to cool.

DATE AND OAT FINGERS

These fingers are particularly high in fibre as they contain oats, whole wheat flour, dates and nuts. Use dried figs or prunes instead of dates sometimes for a change.

*250 g (8 oz) dried chopped
    dates
3 tablespoons apple juice
175 ml (¾ cup) sunflower
    oil
4 tablespoons liquid honey*

*175 g (6 oz) rolled oats
375 ml (1½ cups) whole
    wheat flour
50 g (2 oz) walnuts,
    chopped*

**Makes 14
Preparation time:**
15 minutes
Cooking time:
35 minutes
Freezing:
Recommended

1. Grease and line a 20 cm (8 inch) square shallow cake pan.
2. Place the dates and apple juice in a small pan and simmer for about 5 minutes, until soft.
3. Place the oil and honey in a saucepan and stir over low heat until evenly blended. Add the oats, flour and walnuts and mix together thoroughly.
4. Turn half the mixture into the prepared pan, pressing down firmly.
5. Cover evenly with the date mixture, sprinkle over the remaining oat mixture and press down firmly with a palette knife.
6. Bake in a preheated oven, 190°C/375°F, for 35 minutes, until golden brown.
7. Leave to cool for 5 minutes, then cut into 14 fingers. Allow to cool completely before removing the fingers carefully from the pan.

HONEY APPLE CAKE

Use dessert apples for natural sweetness, and grate the skin for extra fibre and texture.

*500 ml (2 cups) whole wheat
    flour
2 teaspoons baking
    powder
2 teaspoons ground mixed
    spice
3 tablespoons liquid honey
250 g (8 oz) dried chopped
    dates*

*2 eggs
125 ml (½ cup) apple juice
125 ml (½ cup) sunflower
    oil
250 g (8 oz) eating apples,
    cored and grated
2 tablespoons chopped
    hazelnuts*

SUNFLOWER CRUNCHIES

375 ml (1 1/2 cups) rolled oats   *125 ml (1/2 cup) sunflower*
50 ml (1/4 cup) sunflower   *oil*
    seeds, roasted   *1 egg, beaten*
4 tablespoons liquid honey   *1 tablespoon sesame seeds*

Makes about 20
Preparation time:
15 minutes
Cooking time:
15 minutes
Freezing:
Recommended

1. Place all the ingredients in a mixing bowl and mix together thoroughly.
2. Place teaspoonfuls of the mixture well apart on a baking sheet and flatten with a dampened palette knife.
3. Bake in a preheated oven, 180°C/350°F, for 15 minutes, until golden brown.
4. Leave to cool for 2 minutes, then transfer to a wire rack to cool completely.

APRICOT AND ALMOND TARTLETS

Moist and fruity little tartlets, ideal to keep in the freezer as they thaw in about 15 minutes.

FOR THE PASTRY: *50 ml (1/4 cup) whole*
50 ml (1/4 cup) margarine   *wheat flour*
2 tablespoons water   *50 g (2 oz) ground*
250 ml (1 cup) whole wheat   *almonds*
    flour   *few drops almond extract*
FOR THE FILLING: *75 g (3 oz) dried apricots,*
50 ml (1/4 cup) margarine   *chopped and soaked for*
2 tablespoons liquid honey   *2 hours*
1 egg   *25 g (1 oz) sliced almonds*

Makes 14
Preparation time:
30 minutes, plus
soaking and
chilling time
Cooking time:
20 minutes
Freezing:
Recommended

1. Place the margarine, water and 2 tablespoons of the flour in a mixing bowl and blend with a fork. Add the remaining flour and mix together to form a stiff dough.
2. Turn onto a floured surface and knead lightly until smooth. Chill for 20 minutes.
3. To prepare the filling, mix the margarine, honey, egg, flour, ground almonds and extract together until blended. Drain the apricots and dry on paper towels, then mix into the almond mixture.
4. Roll out the pastry very thinly, cut into 7.5 cm (3 inch) rounds and use to line 14 tartlet pans.
5. Spoon the filling into the pastry cases, sprinkle with the flaked almonds and bake in a preheated oven, 190°C/375°F, for 20–25 minutes. Serve warm or cold.

POPPY SEED ROLLS

These are ideal to serve when crusty bread is called for, and they look more attractive than plain whole wheat bread. Sesame seeds can also be used for a change.

1 L (4 cups) whole wheat flour
1 teaspoon salt
1 teaspoon fresh yeast
300 ml (1¼ cups) warm water

1 tablespoon malt extract
1 tablespoon oil
2 tablespoons poppy seeds
beaten egg to glaze

Makes 14
Preparation time:
30 minutes, plus rising time
Cooking time:
15–20 minutes
Freezing:
Recommended

1. Make the dough as for Whole wheat Bread*, adding 1 tablespoon of the poppy seeds instead of the sesame seeds. Leave to rise, then turn out onto a floured surface and knead for 3 minutes.
2. Cut into 14 pieces and shape into rolls. Place on a floured baking sheet, cover with a clean cloth and leave in a warm place until almost doubled in size.
3. Brush with beaten egg and sprinkle with the remaining poppy seeds. Bake in a preheated oven, 220°C/425°F, for 15–20 minutes, until golden. Cool on a rack.

CUMIN CRACKERS

Ideal biscuits to serve with cheese or, made smaller, to serve with dips or plain with drinks.

500 ml (2 cups) whole wheat flour
1 teaspoon baking powder
1 teaspoon ground cumin
3 tablespoons oil

25 g (1 oz) Parmesan cheese, grated
1 tablespoon shoyu or soy sauce
4–5 tablespoons milk
2 teaspoons poppy seeds

Makes about 30
Preparation time:
15 minutes
Cooking time:
10–15 minutes
Freezing:
Recommended

1. Place the flour in a mixing bowl, then sift in the baking powder and cumin. Add the cheese, oil, shoyu or soy sauce, and enough milk to mix to a soft dough.
2. Turn out onto a floured surface, knead lightly, then roll out very thinly. Prick all over with a fork and cut into 7.5 cm (3 inch) rounds with a plain cutter.
3. Place on a baking sheet, brush lightly with water, then sprinkle with the poppy seeds.
4. Bake in a preheated oven, 190°C/375°F, for 10–15 minutes. Transfer to a wire rack to cool.

BASIC RECIPES

WHOLE WHEAT PANCAKES

These pancakes have far more flavour than those made with white flour. You can also use buckwheat flour, which Bretons usually use in their crêpes.

1 egg
300 ml (1¼ cups) milk

250 ml (1 cup) whole
wheat flour

Makes 12–14
Preparation time:
10 minutes, plus
standing time
Cooking time:
15 minutes
Freezing:
Recommended

1. Place the egg and milk in a blender or food processor, add the flour and work for 30 seconds until smooth. Leave to stand for 30 minutes, to thicken.
2. Grease a 15 cm (6 inch) omelette pan and place over a moderate heat. Pour in 1 tablespoon of the batter, tilting the pan to coat the bottom evenly.
3. Cook until the underside is brown, then turn over and cook for 10 seconds.
4. Turn onto a plate and repeat with the remaining batter to make about 12 pancakes. Stack them interleaved with waxed paper and keep warm.

WHOLE WHEAT PASTRY

A simple pastry to make and far less crumbly than the results achieved with the conventional method; therefore it can be rolled out more thinly.

50 ml (¼ cup) margarine
50 ml (¼ cup) shortening
3 tablespoons iced water

500 ml (2 cups) whole
wheat flour

Makes a 250 g
(8 oz) quantity
Preparation time:
8 minutes, plus
chilling
Freezing:
Recommended

1. Place the fats, water and a quarter of the flour in a mixing bowl and mix with a fork until blended.
2. Add the remaining flour and mix to a firm dough.
3. Turn onto a floured surface and knead lightly until smooth, then chill for 20 minutes.
4. Roll the pastry out thinly and use as desired.

VARIATION
Cheese Pastry: Mix in 75 g (3 oz) finely grated old Cheddar cheese and 1 teaspoon sifted dry mustard when adding the remaining flour.

WHOLE WHEAT BREAD

A good basic brown bread to start with. Try making different breads by replacing some of the wheat flour with other grain flours. You can also add oatmeal, malted wheat grains and flaked grains to give different textures, and sesame, poppy, caraway or fennel seeds for different flavours. Fresh yeast can be obtained from most bakeries.

1.5 kg (3 lb) whole wheat flour
1 tablespoon salt
25 g (1 oz) fresh yeast
900 ml (3²/₃ cups) warm water
2 tablespoons malt extract
2 tablespoons oil
1 tablespoon sesame seeds

1. Grease four 1.5 L (8 × 4 inch) loaf pans.
2. Mix the flour and salt together in a bowl. Mix the yeast with a little of the water and leave until frothy.
3. Add to the flour with the remaining water, the malt extract and oil and mix to a dough.
4. Turn onto a floured surface and knead for 8 minutes, until smooth and elastic. Return to the bowl, cover with a damp cloth and leave to rise in a warm place for about 2 hours, until doubled in size.
5. Turn out onto a floured surface, knead for a few minutes, then divide into 4 pieces. Shape and place in the prepared pans. Make diagonal cuts across the surface, brush with water and sprinkle with the sesame seeds.
6. Cover and leave in a warm place for about 30 minutes, until the dough just reaches the top of the pans.
7. Bake in a preheated oven, 220°C/425°F, for 10 minutes, then lower the temperature to 190°C/375°F, and bake for 20–25 minutes, until the bread sounds hollow when tapped. Cool on a wire rack.

Makes four 1.5 L (8 × 4 inch) loaves
Preparation time: 15 minutes, plus rising time
Cooking time: 30–35 minutes
Freezing: Recommended

VARIATIONS

Rye Bread: Replace 500 g (1 lb) of the whole wheat flour with rye flour; the malt extract with molasses; and the sesame seeds with caraway seeds. Shape the dough into 2 oval loaves and place on floured baking sheets. Stab with a fork in about 8 places.

Buckwheat Bread: Replace 500 g (1 lb) of the whole wheat flour with buckwheat flour and add 125 g (4 oz) whole roasted buckwheat with the flours. Shape the dough into 2 round loaves and place on floured baking sheets. Sprinkle with roasted buckwheat instead of sesame seeds.

FRENCH DRESSING

If you cannot obtain concentrated apple juice, substitute 1 teaspoon liquid honey instead. This dressing will keep for several weeks, so it's a good idea to make this quantity.

300 ml (1¼ cups) olive oil
3 tablespoons cider
  vinegar
2 tablespoons
  concentrated apple juice

1 clove garlic, crushed
1½ teaspoons
  coarse-grain mustard
salt and pepper to taste

**Makes 450 ml
(1¾ cups)
Preparation time:**
5 minutes

1. Put the ingredients in a screw-topped jar; shake well.

VARIATION
Herb Vinaigrette: Add 2 tablespoons chopped mixed herbs – such as mint, parsley, thyme, chives.

SHOYU DRESSING

Shoyu is a sauce obtained by naturally fermenting soya beans with wheat or barley. Unlike soy sauce, it contains no artificial flavourings or sugar.

250 ml (1 cup) safflower
  oil
3 tablespoons shoyu
2 cloves garlic, crushed

3 tablespoons cider
  vinegar
pepper to taste

**Makes 300 ml
(1¼ cups)
Preparation time:**
5 minutes

1. Put all the ingredients in a screw-topped jar and shake well to blend.

CORIANDER AND YOGURT SAUCE

A pungent, spicy creamy sauce, good with pulse dishes.

150 ml (²⁄₃ cup) yogurt
1 teaspoon ground
  coriander
1 clove garlic, crushed

1 teaspoon tomato paste
1 teaspoon chopped
  coriander leaves
salt and pepper to taste

**Makes 150 ml
(²⁄₃ cup)
Preparation time:**
5 minutes
Freezing:
Not recommended

1. Place all the ingredients in a small bowl and mix together thoroughly.
2. Serve cold, or heat through gently if you prefer.

WATERCRESS SAUCE

A lovely fresh sauce that tastes particularly good with fish dishes.

1 bunch watercress   *1 clove garlic, crushed*
2 mint sprigs   *1 teaspoon lemon juice*
150 ml (²/₃ cup) yogurt   *salt and pepper to taste*

1. Blanch the watercress and mint in boiling water for 2 minutes; drain well.
2. Chop roughly, then place in a blender or food processor with the yogurt, garlic, lemon juice, and salt and pepper and work until smooth.
3. Serve cold, or heat through gently if you prefer.

Makes 300 ml
(1¼ cups)
Preparation time:
10 minutes
Freezing:
Not recommended

TOMATO SAUCE

A versatile sauce which enhances nut loaves, pasta and many other savoury dishes. If you cannot obtain fresh basil, use another fresh herb—such as parsley or chervil—instead.

1 tablespoon olive oil   *398 ml (14 oz) can*
1 onion, chopped   *tomatoes*
2 cloves garlic, crushed   *1 tablespoon tomato paste*
1 tablespoon whole wheat   *1 tablespoon chopped basil*
*   flour*   *salt and pepper to taste*
150 ml (²/₃ cup) water

1. Heat the oil in a pan, add the onion and fry until softened.
2. Add the garlic and mix in the flour, then stir in the water, tomatoes, tomato paste, and salt and pepper.
3. Bring to the boil, cover and simmer for 20 minutes, stirring occasionally.
4. Cool slightly, then place in a blender or food processor with the basil and work until smooth. Reheat when required.

Makes 350 ml
(1½ cups)
Preparation time:
15 minutes
Cooking time:
20 minutes
Freezing:
Recommended

High Fibre Sources

This table lists the valuable sources of fibre, which you will hopefully find useful when trying to increase the fibre content of your diet.

To give a realistic value, the amount of fibre in each item has been calculated according to how much you might eat in an individual serving. The values are worked out on the presumption that all the edible skins on potatoes, apples, pears, plums, etc, would be eaten, and that any vegetables would be trimmed and prepared in the normal way. All foods are raw unless otherwise stated.

Consequently foods with over 6 grams of fibre per serving are considered excellent sources; those with over 4 grams of fibre are very good sources and useful sources have over 2 grams of fibre per serving.

EXCELLENT SOURCES (more than 6.0 grams fibre per serving)

Item	Weight of serving	Item	Weight of serving
VEGETABLES		**FRUIT**	
Baked beans in	225 g (8 oz)	Apricots, dried	50 g (2 oz)
tomato		Blackberries	100 g (3½ oz)
sauce		Blackcurrants	100 g (3½ oz)
Beans, dried		Figs, dried	50 g (2 oz)
(including		Loganberries	100 g (3½ oz)
black, black		Prunes, dried	50 g (2 oz)
eye, butter,	40 g (1½ oz)	Raspberries	100 g (3½ oz)
mung, pinto,			
red kidney,		**GRAINS, NUTS AND SEEDS**	
white kidney)		Breakfast Bran	50 g (2 oz)
Chick peas, dried	50 g (2 oz)		
Peas, frozen	75 g (3 oz)		
Peas, dried	50 g (2 oz)		
Peas, split and			
dried	50 g (2 oz)		

VERY GOOD SOURCES (more than 4.0 grams fibre per serving)

Item	Weight of serving	Item	Weight of serving
VEGETABLES		Dates, dried	50 g (2 oz)
Beans, broad	100 g (3½ oz)	Figs, fresh	250 g (8 oz)
Broccoli	100 g (3½ oz)	Passion fruit	25 g (1 oz)
Kernel corn	100 g (3½ oz)		
Lentils	50 g (2 oz)	**GRAINS, NUTS AND SEEDS**	
Peas, fresh	100 g (3½ oz)	Bread, whole wheat	70 g (2½ oz)–
Potato, baked	200 g (7 oz)		2 slices
Snow Peas	100 g (3½ oz)	Flour, whole wheat	50 g (2 oz)
		Muesli	50 g (2 oz)
FRUIT		Pasta, whole wheat	
Cranberries	100 g (3½ oz)	(dried)	50 g (2 oz)
Damsons	100 g (3½ oz)		

USEFUL SOURCES (more than 2.0 grams fibre per serving)

Item	Weight of serving	Item	Weight of serving
VEGETABLES		Oranges	1 average-sized
Beans, green	100 g (3½ oz)	Pears	1 average-sized
Beans, runner	100 g (3½ oz)	Pears, dried	25 g (1 oz)
Bean sprouts	100 g (3½ oz)	Plums, Victoria	100 g (3½ oz)
Brussels sprouts	100 g (3½ oz)	Rhubarb	100 g (3½ oz)
Cabbage (red, savoy, spring, white)	100 g (3½ oz)	Strawberries	100 g (3½ oz)
Carrots	100 g (3½ oz)	**GRAINS, NUTS AND SEEDS**	
Cauliflower	100 g (3½ oz)	Almonds	25 g (1 oz)
Celery	100 g (3½ oz)	Barley flakes	25 g (1 oz)
Egg plant	100 g (3½ oz)	Buckwheat flakes	25 g (1 oz)
Leeks	100 g (3½ oz)	Bulgur wheat	50 g (2 oz)
Mushrooms	100 g (3½ oz)	Brazil nuts	25 g (1 oz)
Parsley	25 g (1 oz)	Bread, brown	70 g (2½ oz)– 2 slices
Parsnips	100 g (3½ oz)	Cashew nuts	25 g (1 oz)
Zucchini	125 g (4 oz)	Coconut, desiccated	25 g (1 oz)
FRUIT		Coconut, fresh	50 g (2 oz)
Apple	1 average-sized	Hazelnuts	50 g (2 oz)
Apple, dried	25 g (1 oz)	Oatmeal	50 g (2 oz)
Apricots, fresh	100 g (3½ oz)	Oats, rolled	50 g (2 oz)
Avocado	½ average-sized	Pine nuts	15 g (½ oz)
Banana	1 average-sized	Poppy seeds	15 g (½ oz)
Gooseberries	100 g (3½ oz)	Pumpkin seeds	15 g (½ oz)
Grapes	175 g (6 oz)	Rice, brown	50 g (2 oz)
Greengages	100 g (3½ oz)	Sesame seeds	15 g (½ oz)
Nectarines	1 average-sized	Sunflower seeds	15 g (½ oz)
Olives	50 g (2 oz)	Wheat flakes	25 g (1 oz)

Cooking Time Guide for Pulses

The longer beans have been kept in a dry place the longer they will take to cook. It is not possible to be exact with cooking times therefore, but this approximate guide should be useful.

Item	Time	Item	Time
Aduki beans	40–45 minutes	Kidney beans	1¼–1½ hours
Black beans	1½ hours	Mung beans	30–45 minutes
Black eye beans	30–45 minutes	Pinto beans	1 hour
Butter beans	45 minutes	Chick peas	1 hour
Flageolet beans	40–45 minutes	Green lentils	45–50 minutes
Haricot beans	1¼–1½ hours	Red lentils	20–30 minutes

INDEX

Photography by: Clive Streeter
Designed by: Sue Storey
Home economist: Carole Handslip
Stylist: Gina Carminati
Jacket photograph by: Paul Williams
Illustration by: Linda Smith
Typeset by Rowland Phototypesetting Ltd